TABLE OF CONTENTS

CHAPTER ONE

MINDFULNESS

Mindfulness denotes an attitude of care, presence, and awareness, which may be internal (feelings, thoughts, emotions, actions, motivations, etc.) or external (surrounding world, sounds, objects, events, etc.).

It is an ancient Indian notion, "right attention." This is associated with Siddhartha Gautama's teaching. It plays an important role in Buddhism, where mindfulness is a necessary step towards liberation, known as Bodhi or spiritual awakening; one of the noble eightfold path members.

Scientific publications on the subject are of uneven quality, possibly based on methodological biases or conflicts of interest. The systematic analysis of well-conducted research shows weak to moderate effects on psychological stress (anxiety, depression, and pain), while on many other disorders, no significant effect is demonstrated. Some also assert that although proclaimed secular, mindfulness remains attached to Buddhism and that there are risks of instrumentalism by various structures such as companies, armies, or even sectarian groups. However, it remains clear that 'mindfulness' has become a commonplace phrase. So, why is this?

Right attention or mindfulness consists of returning one's attention to the present moment and observing the sensations or thoughts as they appear and then disappear: it is the attention paid to life and its experience, without filter (we accept what comes our way), without judgment (we do not decide whether it is good or bad, desirable or not) and without waiting (we are not looking for something specific).

The practitioner can examine matter (especially the body), perceptions, positive or negative mental habits and consciousness. The observer aims to remain neutral and "mentally silent" by examining the appearance and disappearance of pleasant, neutral, or unpleasant sensations, without judging, without seeking to retain the pleasant sensation or reject the unpleasant sensation. In a Buddhist approach, the observer learns to detach and gradually frees himself from matter, sensation, perception, mental conditionings, consciousness, and suffering (known as "Dukkha").

This mindfulness is not limited to the practice of meditation, but it is simply to observe the physical and mental objects that present themselves to the mind. When an object disappears, mindfulness does not cease; the observer turns it towards a "default" object: the breath or the walk. When a new object appears in the mind, attention leaves the "default" object. It applies itself to observing the new object according to both aspects of its nature, as conventional truth (Sammuti Sacca) and as the ultimate truth (Parramatta, Sacca). Attention to the breath (ānāpānasati): inhale, small pause, exhale, small pause, is not an end in itself, but it effectively supports the vitality of mindfulness.

The Buddha advises to observe sensation internally (which means observing it in mind) and externally (observing it in the body). For example, if the observer sees in the mind: "hot," he can also see dilation of blood vessels and sweating in the body. If the observer sees in the mind: "cold," he can also see the contraction of blood vessels and shivering in the body.

Mindfulness is beyond the first form of wisdom: the aspiration of listening or reading instructions, and beyond the second form: the logic of the intellect. It is the third form of wisdom, known as Bhavana-Maya Panna; the direct vision of the ultimate reality in all things, the wisdom obtained by direct personal experience, and the mind's development.

The goal of mindfulness is to learn to control and manage our mind and focus on our experience. Through this ability, we self-regulate our attention to remain fully aware of the present moment; of what we are experiencing.

All human beings have this mental capacity that we could take great advantage of for our benefit. If there is currently a multitude of research being done in this regard, it is because it has been proven that this mental attitude influences our management of emotions, our behavior and, consequently, our mental and physical health.

Although it sounds simple to us, paying attention to our experiences, in our way of living that we have learnt, it is quite difficult for us to incorporate this mental attitude in our day to day life. We currently live in a world of information and technology, the stimuli are constant, and we have accustomed our mind to being on many tasks simultaneously. With this frenetic pace of life that we live, it is not surprising that our concentration is affected, and not only our concentration but also the way we serve ourselves.

We constantly suffer and worry about circumstances that are part of our existence. We strive to retain past situations, moments and emotions. We worry and anticipate the pain of situations that we fear. This makes us live continuously in our past and future, and it happens that we become unable to attend to our experience from the present.

Mindfulness has crept into our lives almost without warning. This practice has aroused people's interest from all walks of life due to its positive effects on our well-being.

However, although this is a more or less recent trend for most of us, the truth is that it has centuries of history; specifically, its beginnings are linked to the appearance of Buddhism at the end of the 7th century BC.

Its success is in the benefits that mindfulness produces in our mind and our body. It subsequently helps us manage our emotions, reactions, and thoughts; to control them via acceptance and freedom. It is a way of connecting with our inner self to calmly face day-to-day challenges such as anxiety, stress, suffering, and the problem that concerns us today, which is insomnia.

Mindfulness consists of directing our focus or attention towards what interests us, to extract the appreciation and value of that experience that we are experiencing. It is about learning to direct, stabilize and increase the potential of our attention. Consequently, we will obtain mental clarity, allowing us to see beyond each person, each situation and each experience. Our range of attention expands, and we do not get stuck in the narrowness of our thoughts. The possibilities and prospects are widening.

To understand it better, we can use the metaphor of water that rots when it stagnates. Our thoughts also rot when we do not let them flow; when we insist on bringing the same thoughts repeatedly to our mind (rumination), causing us suffering and even mood disorders such as depression.

This often means that this flow of thoughts stagnates when we do not control our attention or concentration towards what we live. Mindfulness helps us get out of that loop so that we cannot be distracted by the thoughts that prevent us from seeing our experiences with transparency and depth. Thus, we manage to remove the sedimented earth to see the bottom and the contents of the pond.

THE COMPONENTS OF MINDFULNESS

The components of mindfulness which come from Zen teachings are the following:

1. Attention to the present moment: Focus on the present moment instead of being aware of the past or the future (expectations, desires, and fears). There are divergent opinions as to whether attention should be directed to internal processes or to events in daily life. However, it is possible to reconcile these divergent approaches. While meditating, you can attend to your own internal processes and, in everyday life, focus on the task at hand.

2. Openness to experience: Ability to observe the experience without interposing the filter of one's own beliefs. In other words, observing the experience as if it were the first time, a quality that in Zen is called "beginner's mind." It also implies being open to a negative experience and observing what happens with curiosity.

3. Acceptance: Acceptance can be defined as experiencing events fully and without defenses, as they are; not resisting the flow of life. People engage in maladaptive behaviors in an attempt to avoid unpleasant experiences, but by accepting that these experiences are occasional and limited in time, they will not need to resort to such behaviors.

4. Let go: It consists of detaching ourselves from something to which we clung. One of our ego's characteristics is to try to treasure things, relationships, power, and money. It is mistakenly believed that the more you own, the more you control yourself, the more you get, the happier you will be. The desire to cling collides with a basic characteristic of reality, which is the temporality of things. Nothing in the material world is stable for a long time; everything persists for a certain time and then perishes.

5. Intention: It is what each person pursues when practicing mindfulness. This might sound contradictory to one of the mindfulness attitudes, which is not striving for any purpose. When you are meditating, you should not try to achieve any immediate purpose; you simply have to participate with full awareness of what you are

doing. However, you also have to have a purpose, a personal goal, to move towards that purpose.

PHYSICAL CONDITIONS TO PRACTICE MINDFULNESS

- Right place

Although any site can be turned into a suitable place, this place must be one that you choose carefully. A place where you know that you will always be able to go and be calm without external distractions of any kind. A place reserved for you, which you can accommodate to your liking: with the light that you find most comfortable, the decoration and the environment in which you want to relax; symbolic objects, candles, plants. A place that you adapt with great care to your comfort and taste.

Ensure, if possible, that this place is away from noise and possible interruptions. The objective is that you are as calm and comfortable as possible in that place you have chosen.

- Choose your moment

Practicing once or twice in a day is advisable. When to do it? You choose those times of the day: there is nothing regulated as to what time of day is the best. The most appropriate is the one that you decide is best for you.

To do this, first answer one question: "At what time of day do I feel best?" Avoid times when you are very tired and sleepy. For example, it is not advisable after a copious meal, nor before going to bed if you arrive at that moment very tired after daily tasks. Try not to think of this practice as to promote sleep, but rather to wake up, focusing all your energy to mindfulness.

This time you choose; try to make it one you can use every day so that it is easier for you to acquire a daily discipline.

- Comfortable posture

Try to use a stable posture, in which you can stay for a long time without tiring or causing you discomfort. The purpose of proper posture is to get you away from discomfort and decrease your muscle tension. This means that you can free yourself from the discomfort that your body generates as soon as possible, so you do not get distracted from mindfulness. If you are unfamiliar with meditation postures, try various postures until you find the most comfortable and suitable one.

- Timer

If you are starting with mindfulness, it is recommended that you use a timer, enabling you to know when it is time to conclude your practice without worrying about time, without becoming distracted thinking about how much will remain, or if you have already exceeded the one you had proposed.

More experienced practitioners can do without this, but it is highly recommended for beginners to set time in order to not worry themselves on it.

These conditions are simple to follow, and yet they form vital steps towards practicing mindfulness effectively.

MINDFULNESS EXERCISES

One of the first things you learn when you start mindfulness training is how oblivious we can be. Harvard research has demonstrated that our minds deviate from the present moment about half of the time. So, we are not fully present for half of our waking life. The wandering mind seems to be the default state of our brain; the brain circuit that is active when our mind is wandering is called the "default mode network" since it activates when we are not engaged in a particular task. The good news is that the practice of mindfulness meditation seems to limit the activation of this network. This corroborates the testimony we often hear that people feel more centered and present when they begin to meditate.

The following exercises can help develop mindfulness techniques:

- Choose an object that you have around you and fix your attention on that object for a single minute. Ignore everything else and feel like there is only you and that object in that room. Look at it as if you were looking at it for the first time. Look at the nuances. Embrace the naive attitude of the child who observes reality with the novelty of surprise that produces pleasant emotions. Connect with that state of childhood illusion because that inner child still lives in your heart.

- Walk barefoot along the edge of the beach or across the park lawn. Feet receive little stimulation from being protected by a stiff shoe during winter, so the pleasure of walking barefoot is a simple mindfulness routine thanks to the sensory input you receive. But in addition, you also experience contact with the therapeutic power of nature.

- You can use different anchors, not just visual, as in the case of observing a physical object for a minute. You can also use auditory stimuli to focus your mindfulness and create a mood. For example, practice a relaxation exercise using soothing music. In this way, that melody always inspires you with emotions of serenity and peace by establishing a cause and effect relationship. That is, you turn this stimulus into a force engine for you.

- Practice alternate breathing. For instance, take three alternate breaths; covering one side or the other of the nose in each case. Continue for one minute, focusing your full attention solely on your breathing. Take only three such breaths and stop if you experience any discomfort or dizziness: some people have difficulty breathing through their nose.

- Listen to the sounds of nature. Let's say, the sound of river water, the song of birds or the wind that caresses your skin. Walk through a natural environment, offering your complete attention to those stimuli that make you experience the transcendent connection with everything that exists. A natural space is a particularly advisable setting to experience mindfulness thanks to the inimitable beauty of the natural world.

- Hug a loved one and feel how your own universe of positive communication is established between you. That is, experience the positive energy of body language in the form of love. A hug is a metaphor for mindfulness since your mind, and your body is activated through this expression of affection with which you receive doses of self-esteem in the form of a present.

- Read poetry out loud. The cadence and musicality of a poem surround your mind in an atmosphere of aesthetic emotions. Read a poem with a pause, trying to understand what the poet expresses in each verse.

- Is there a place you relish in visiting because it gives you a feeling of calm and serenity? Where do you find the refuge of silence? Make a list of spaces which feel like your own thanks to a cozy silence. Those spaces are those in which your mood is most receptive to mindfulness. In other words, places produce emotions. For this reason, when you feel embraced by a space, your heart expands in the form of mindfulness. Practicing mindfulness at home is almost certainly a good starting point.

- Look in the mirror while you breathe deeply. Look into your eyes in the reflection of the glass. Relish this bond of friendship with yourself. You can also dedicate a few words to carry out this practice of mindfulness through internal dialogue with yourself. You can put into practice the message of Thich Nhat Hanh, an expert in personal transformation who explains how when you take care of your inner child; you experience a reunion with yourself.

WHAT THE FUTURE HOLDS FOR MINDFULNESS

The practice of mindfulness promises many positive changes around the world. It is said that a person who meditates becomes a better human being, which, in turn, positively impacts the individual and their environment. This is perhaps somewhat of a cure for the 21st century's epidemic of stress and the world's situation in general.

Organizations of such importance as the NICABM (National Institute for the Clinical Application of Behavioral Medicine) promote the integration of mindfulness in traditional conversation therapies. According to studies, 66% of people who go to psychotherapy do not show any significant improvement, not because of the incapacity of the professionals, but because of the lack of emotional commitment of the patients. In this context, with overwhelming results, mindfulness has proven to alter this trend rapidly, encouraging patients to participate with commitment, intention and responsibly in their transformation process.

HOW TO INCREASE PRODUCTIVITY THROUGH MINDFULNESS

In these times in which we live, overwhelmed with interruptions and distractions, it is increasingly necessary to control our attention muscle to respond to the whirlwind of day to day occurrences. It is often considered that the solution has to come from reducing human structures and increasing the weight of the technology. But what if the solutions came from other proposals? What if they came from our ability to silence ourselves, observe ourselves, and manage ourselves with a conscience?

Being a practice that does not impregnate any dogma, religion or belief, more and more corporations around the world are developing mindfulness training programs to improve the happiness and well-being of employees. Numerous scientific studies support and demonstrate its positive impact on our brain, the most powerful organ we have, and the most significant in it's potential to transform us into effective and successful professionals. Those same studies support that the continued practice of mindfulness is associated with the development of brain areas that increase the ability to handle conflicts, achieve higher levels of concentration and offer a conscious response in high pressure situations.

Let us look at the aspects of productivity which mindfulness practice helps to improve:

Mental clarity: In the dynamics of today's world, dispersion, multitasking and the lack of clarity about what one really must do, we have installed what many refer to as "survival management," with disastrous consequences for productivity. Mindfulness develops the necessary capacity to concentrate and focus on what is truly important from a calm and confident mind.

Emotional intelligence: The ability to regulate our emotions is already an essential skill recognised by all human resources experts. Mindfulness offers our brain systematic training to live our emotions with full attention, without escapism and manage them towards healthier and more conscious behaviors. Reactive behaviors decrease to give way to conscious and assertive responses.

Strategic vision: With the practice of Mindfulness, our brain is trained to eliminate the mental noise that disperses and blocks the management capacity from excellence to organize, plan and make decisions that are beneficial and productive in the long term.

Creativity and innovation: True creativity comes from a silenced mind. It is impossible to create and find inspired solutions with a mind full of noise. The moment we practice Mindfulness, we train the mind to find serenity and calm, and that emptiness is where inspiration, innovation, and creativity can be born to solve complex situations in the business maelstrom.

Stress management: The effectiveness of this technique in reducing stress levels to at least 78% due to anxiety, stress or depression has been detected in companies that carry out this practice. The continuous practice of mindfulness does not only help to reduce stress levels but also helps recovery periods from stressful situations as we know that a clear and present mind is much more efficient than a stressed mind.

CHAPTER TWO

MINDFULNESS AND SCIENCE

For the past thirty years, science has been interested in meditation and has sought to explain its cognitive and emotional benefits, and more generally, its positive impact on health. The research field has made it possible to explain better the interconnection between body, mind, brain, subjective experience and well-being. Scientists have thus tried to provide evidence for what contemplatives have been describing for millennia. This evolution of research owes a lot to the emergence of Mindfulness-based approaches that appeared in the medical sector in the late 1970s.

When we meditate by staying focused on the breath, we train our brains to live in the present and ward off any restlessness. Our attention is focused on the one thing, and little by little, we are entering a state of relaxation and peace.

Perhaps the most important reason that mindfulness has become a mainstream health-promoting intervention - in addition to a popular lifestyle - is the dramatic increase in scientific research on mindfulness over the past decade. The following is an overview of some of the most interesting and surprising results in this area of research.

- Neuroplasticity

Recent advances in psychology and neuroscience have shown that mental health, well-being, and emotional balance are skills that can be developed through practice.

This hypothesis has been confirmed more recently by neuroscientists. Neuroplasticity is the idea that the brain is an organ of experience that is constantly evolving and reshaping itself to adapt to everyday life demands. Before this paradigm shift, researchers viewed the brain as relatively fixed. There is a lot of evidence that the structure and function of the brain changes depending on what we do.

Let's say you want to learn to juggle; you will have to repeat the gestures repeatedly until they become automatic. The development of this skill results in structural and functional changes in the motor cortex, a structure in the upper layer of the brain, near the top of the head that controls the body's movement. An interesting study explains that London taxi drivers have larger-than-average hippocampus. The hippocampus is one of the structures in the brain that stores spatial maps. London is a huge city with complex ramifications, and drivers need to know it inside out. Drivers continually use their space maps to navigate the city, and their hippocampus becomes larger.

- The brain changes with the practice of mindfulness

Neuroplasticity is of particular appeal to those who want to improve their mental health, well-being, and performance. 15 years ago, a brain imaging study of Buddhist monks disclosed measurable differences between monks' brains and those of people of Western descent, suggesting that thousands of hours of meditation practice could demonstrably change the way we see life. During these tests, a monk was meditating on compassion in a scanner and the researchers recorded brain activity 30 times greater than anything previously captured using this technology.

A follow-up study showed that monks' brains' differences don't just depend on their particular lifestyle: living in the jungle, without a job, without a family or a mortgage. Changes in the brain's structure and function have been observed in ordinary people who have completed an eight-week training course called Mindfulness-Based Stress Reduction (MBSR), which involves the daily practice of meditation. It has been shown that through this practice, the amygdala, a brain structure that processes fear and anxiety, shrinks. The frontal lobes, responsible for planning, thinking, and problem solving thicken; the island lobe, which acts on self-awareness, also develops.

The benefits of mindfulness meditation are also manifested in other aspects of our physiological makeup. Meditation can improve our immune system's efficiency, significantly reduce the stress hormone cortisol, and reduce inflammation in the body.

THE SCIENTIFIC ROOTS OF MINDFULNESS

Designed by Jon Kabat-Zinn, doctor of molecular biology, the MBSR program has been part of the mainstream of integrative medicine since its creation in 1979 at the Massachusetts Faculty of Medicine. It has been the subject of much research to assess and objectify its benefits. Its structured and relatively reproducible format, and its positive impact on health quickly caught the scientific community's attention. This is how psychology professors Zindel Segal, John Teasdale, and Mark Williams became interested in meditative practice as part of their research on depression, giving rise to the MBCT program in the early 2000s.

Numerous studies attest to the health benefits of Mindfulness-based approaches, both in somatic and cognitive conditions. Their effectiveness has thus been established in reducing the symptoms of many disorders, such as stress (including post-traumatic stress), chronic pain, anxiety, depression, insomnia, eating disorders or addictions, as well as in burnout prevention.

Since the early 2000s, the number of Mindfulness-based protocols research has increased dramatically, exceeding 600 recognised studies per year. It is in this context that the American Mindfulness Research Association was created in 2013. This organization, which brings together specialists in Mindfulness research such as Richard Davidson, Rebecca Crane and Mark Williams, has to contribute to the established standards for the research and dissemination of resources.

In early 2018, the creation of a Mindfulness division within the Department of Medicine at the University of Massachusetts, undoubtedly the first university chair entirely dedicated to this field, reaffirmed this institution's ambition to pursue the research on its medical applications at the very place where MBSR was born. This is another strong sign of the acceleration of the recognition of Mindfulness-based approaches by the scientific world, further highlighted by the recent creation of the Mindfulness Center within Brown University, which devotes significant funds to research in this area.

WHAT DOES SCIENCE SAY ABOUT THE MECHANISMS INVOLVED IN MINDFULNESS?

Neuroscience shows to varying degrees, for experts and novices alike, that the practice of meditation alters the brain's function and structure: new neural connections are created, and the volume of gray matter increases in certain areas.

This cerebral plasticity, measured using medical imaging and recordings of brain activity, is characterized in particular by a decrease in the amygdala activity (involved in the processing of emotions such as fear and anxiety.). Also, by increased activation in the insula and the pre-frontal cortex (a region of the brain involved in the processing of attention and the executive functions that control behavior), we see better emotional regulation.

By itself, the insular cortex is involved in many functions of the organism: it participates in particular in interoceptive consciousness, the perception of pain, the awareness of emotions, and the control of autonomic functions by modulating the sympathetic and nervous systems.

The parasympathetic meditative practice promotes the maintenance of the body's homeostasis (stability of the internal environment) by activating the autonomic nervous system's parasympathetic branch, which is sometimes called the relaxation response, detriment of the sympathetic branch, which is activated in reaction to stress. By implementing natural self-regulatory abilities, meditation creates physical and mental conditions that contribute to healing and better health.

Its impact is not observable only in the brain. Neurochemical and other genetic changes are also noticeable. Thus, some well publicised studies seem to show positive effects on inflammatory phenomena, immunity, and cellular aging.

Meditative practices have an action on physiological markers of stress. In particular, they have a role in regulating mood and immune function by impacting the level of certain hormones and neurotransmitters. Thus, overall, meditators observe an increase in dopamine, serotonin, endorphins (hormones related to the feeling of well-being), and a decrease in cortisol and norepinephrine (connected with the stress reaction).

Studies have also measured a decrease in circulating cytokines, markers of inflammation secreted by immune cells. In addition, by influencing the enzymes regulating the reading of the genome, the practice of meditation decreases the expression of genes responsible for inflammatory mechanisms. These alterations can be seen as a sign of better regulation of immune functions with a limitation of pro-inflammatory mechanisms.

Mindfulness meditation also contributes to slowing down aging by promoting the activity of telomerase, an enzyme that contributes to the lengthening of telomeres, the DNA segments located at the end of chromosomes and whose length is correlated with cellular aging.

THE BENEFITS OF MINDFULNESS ACCORDING TO SCIENTIFIC PROOF

- Better emotional control and management

The fundamental characteristics and the reason why many people begin to incorporate the practice of mindfulness in their day to day life is that it provides them with a greater management of emotions. That is, it helps to identify the emotion, accept it, cradle it and learn to manage it correctly. Thus, the person practicing begins to master their emotions, and the opposite happens less often; that emotions come to overwhelm the person. Findings show that people who practice mindfulness in their day to day activities have greater self-control compare to those that doesn't.

- Improve ability to concentrate

Bringing our attention to what is happening and bringing it to the present moment is another objective that people consider and finally learn with the continuous and habitual practice of mindfulness. Becoming familiar with mindfulness to the extent that a person has gradually incorporated awareness training, mindfulness and meditation into their day to day life, means that the person will be able to do it with ease and manage to voluntarily direct the mental processes; the ability to concentrate increases, and it becomes easier to notice, and act accordingly on, a distraction that is not useful in daily activities.

- It improves memory capacity.

If the ability to concentrate increase as explained, so does the memory capacity. If the person manages to withdraw their attention from distractions and stay focused, then their memory will naturally perform better. Most of the findings that have addressed this variable conclude that, with the practice of mindfulness, a significant increase in the volume of the gray matter in the human brain is perceived. They also conclude that there is an increase in the size of hippocampus and the cerebral cortex, brain areas that relate to memory and learning.

- It increases relaxation

It has been proven that mindfulness brings calmness, and it is a practice that fills us with tranquility, relaxes body and mind.

- Insomnia reduction

People who practice mindfulness sleep better, but how does this help us?

To put it simply, a state of calmness and an increase in relaxation is reached; this implies that the person feels calmer and without certain worries that steal time. One of the common complaints that people who suffer from insomnia reported to their doctor is that their head begins to work when they lie down in bed. Mindfulness is, in its essence, a means to stop this sensation of the mind working overtime.

HOW OUR BRAIN CHANGES WITH THE PRACTICE OF MINDFULNESS

For a long time, it was believed that we were victims of our physiological inheritance and could not influence it. Today we know that this is not the case, and there is copious scientific evidence to support it.

Recent technological advances in neurofeedback and brain scanning validate that contemplative and meditative practices can improve communication between different brain regions, improving their functions and even creating new neurons, which is called "neurogenesis." While mindfulness's daily practice allows our brain to change, what professionals have called "neuroplasticity", an inadequately stimulating lifestyle (sometimes called the mindlessness state) generates the opposite effect that we know as "neurorigidity".

Why are these changes important? Well, these areas of the brain have a direct influence on our thoughts and behaviors. That is, the quality of your mental content or the way you act under certain circumstances, depend directly on the efficiency of communication between different regions of the brain.

The studies of Sara Lazar, a prestigious neuroscientist who has appeared in publications such as Scientific American, show that the daily practice of mindfulness can shrink the amygdala; the same system that has a key role in the search and detection of danger and fear signs, which may well be real or imaginary. It activates the "flight" mode (sympathetic nervous system) constantly during the day. The amygdala mechanism activates a series of biochemical processes, releasing hormones such as cortisol and adrenaline, which are harmful to the peaceful mind, especially considering that we generally do not know how to activate the opposite mode, which is a state of natural recovery: the parasympathetic nervous system. It is now widely accepted that regular mindfulness practice can have this shrinking effect on the amygdala; now, this is relevant in this era of technological distractions and work stress or burnout, since it promotes the evolution of a fearful and reactive brain. As we do not usually pay attention to the present moment, we allow the wandering or catastrophic mind to take over our focus. This becomes a vicious circle that can seriously affect us if we do not get out of mental rumination and calm our 'catastrophic' awareness from time to time.

CHAPTER THREE

MINDFULNESS-BASED COGNITIVE THERAPY

The Mindfulness-Based Cognitive Therapy program was developed by Zindel Segal, John Teasdale, and Mark Williams in the early 2000s as an adaptation of the MBSR program to which elements of cognitive and behavioral therapy were incorporated in order to prevent a depressive relapse. It is aimed more particularly at people suffering from repeated depression.

The three psychology professors and researchers behind the program have shown that there is increased cognitive responsiveness in people with depression, explaining the increasingly frequent relapses after each episode. The professionals behind MBCT then became interested in mindfulness meditation as a means of distancing their patients from thoughts and, therefore, interrupting the process of ruminations.

The non-acceptance of painful emotional states and the implementation of ineffective strategies to leave these painful states can fuel depressive ruminations and lead to the exhaustion and the feeling of failure that often accompany depression.

During the MBCT program, participants are encouraged to develop qualities of acceptance and to become aware of the patterns that trigger a depressive relapse.

This program combines the practice of meditation with a real education on what depression is and the implementation of concrete strategies when the warning signs of depression are felt.

TYPES OF MINDFULNESS APPLICATION IN COGNITIVE THERAPY

- Mindfulness-Based Stress Reduction or MBSR

Jon Kabat-Zinn develops this in 1979, and the method is now offered in 200 American hospitals. The principle has also been adopted by writers, lecturers, and psychologists in the treatment of stress and anxiety. Mindfulness meditation is an adaptation of the Buddhist meditation mindfulness aimed at combatting anxiety, stress, illness and pain. It is also a technique of well-being that allows individuals to experience the present moment more intensely. According to renowned biostatistician Bruno Falissard, clinical studies on the subject are sufficient to recognize that it is a psychotherapeutic treatment with convincing results.

Mindfulness meditation does not consist of thinking about anything, but rather in redirecting your attention either in a targeted way, towards one or more elements of the present (on your sensations, on your breathing or any other psychological phenomenon such as pain, or well-being), or in a non-targeted way, by opening one's vigilance, and one's senses, to all the elements of the present moment, as and when they enter the scene (noises, thoughts, memories, temperature, projects, feelings, body position). According to Christophe André "In particular, in the face of daily stressful moments, one proposes not to try to escape these moments by distraction (by thinking of something else) or by action (by absorbing oneself in work or leisure); on the contrary, it is a question of welcoming them and observing them, in a particular state of consciousness and bodily awakening which makes it possible to prevent them from worsening or becoming chronic."

By listening to the present and one's own sensations, the meditator is in the presence of the structure of their habits. Thoughts having a major impact on our feeling of well-being and our daily decisions, mindfulness meditation, by putting the practitioner in direct awareness with his sensations in the present moment, will have a calming effect at a minimum.

- Mindfulness-Based Cognitive Therapy for Depression or MBCTD

This was presented to prevent depressive relapse, which, when it becomes regular, leads in many cases to suicide, or attempted suicide. A study from the University of Oxford published in April 2015 by The Lancet shows that therapy based on mindfulness meditation is as effective an alternative treatment with antidepressants to prevent depressive relapse.

The use of mindfulness is based on a "change of postulate". While classical cognitive therapies argued that it was necessary to work on the contents of negative thoughts and cognitive biases, the application of MBCTD to the prevention of depressive relapses is based on results which lead to thinking that vulnerability depends, above all else, on the mood rather than the content of thoughts. The mood is thought to play a major role in contributing to dysfunctional thoughts and depressive relapse.

WHO CAN BENEFIT FROM MINDFULNESS-BASED COGNITIVE THERAPY?

This program is beneficial to anyone looking to learn to relate to unwanted thoughts and feelings in new ways and respond to them intentionally and more adequately.

It is of particular benefit to people who suffer from repeated depression, offering them the opportunity to develop the ability to recognize the first signs of relapse and intervene before negative thought patterns set in and mood symptoms become severe.

Studies have proven the effectiveness of MBCT

- In the reduction of symptoms of depression;
- In the prevention of future depressive episodes for those with repeated depression.
- In support of drug treatment, which can help reduce use.

It is recommended to have a specialized follow-up by a professional of depression to clearly establish the individual effectiveness of this therapy and to evaluate with them the risks of relapse. The program is most effective for patients in remission as it is difficult to follow in a major depressive state. The opinion of the specialist who usually follows the patient is required before enrollment in the program.

CHAPTER FOUR

MINDFULNESS, MEDITATION AND THERAPY

MBSR cognitive therapy is a program of meditation exercises aimed at reducing stress and eliminating anxiety states. Cognitive mindfulness-based therapies derived from MBSR are used in psychiatry. From a positive psychology perspective, mindfulness meditation can be used as a technique for well-being or even personal development.

Cognitive control allows people to keep their attention on important choices and ignore other impulses. Poor planning, distracted attention, and difficulty in suppressing impulse all indicate problems with cognitive control. Now, more and more studies have revealed that strengthening "mental muscles" through so-called mindfulness meditation can help children and adults cope with attention deficit hyperactivity disorder (ADHD, seen in children) and attention deficit disorder (ADD, seen in adults).

Just as people are increasingly disillusioned with the first-line treatment for such diseases, the emergence of these studies comes at the right time.

In 2007, researchers at the University of California, Los Angeles (UCLA) published a study that found the incidence of ADHD and cognitive dysfunction and related mood disorders such as depression among Finnish adolescents was almost exactly the same as among American teenagers. The real difference is that in the

United States, most adolescents with ADHD take medication; in Finland, this is not the case.

Although most adolescents with ADHD generally benefit from such treatment in the first year, the effects usually begin to gradually diminish in the third year or earlier.

Taking ADHD drugs does not bring long-lasting benefits. However, mindfulness meditation seems to train the part of the brain that reduces ADHD activity, and this explains why mindfulness meditation can be so important.

According to many different recognized scientific groups, cognitive control can be defined as delayed gratification, impulse management, emotional self-regulation or self-control, suppression of irrelevant thoughts, concentration or preparation for learning.

Researchers have found that having this extraordinary mental ability often indicates success, whether in school or in work and life.

However, it is pointed out that our level of impulsivity will peak around the age of 16, and most people in their 20s have reached the level of adult cognitive control. In healthy adults, cognitive control abilities begin to significantly weaken at the age of 70 or 80, usually manifested as the inability to remember names or words, because they can no longer suppress their distractions.

Today, experts have suggested that strengthening the mental ability of cognitive control may be particularly helpful in the treatment of ADHD and ADD. On their way to this assertion, researchers tested mindfulness meditation; they taught people to monitor their thoughts and feelings, but neither judge nor react in any way. The researchers found that these exercises did not take the subjects' attention away from the selected target. On the contrary, they became more focused after a while.

A new study shows that a brief introduction to mindfulness can help people cope with physical pain and negative emotions.

They found that the effects of mindfulness were so obvious that even if the participants' forearms were exposed to high temperatures, their brains would react as to normal, or non-extreme, temperatures. Research participants reported that using mindfulness techniques reduced pain and negative emotions.

Mindfulness has shown benefits in the treatment of anxiety and depression. But Hedy Kober, Associate Professor of Psychiatry and of Psychology at Yale University and her colleagues wanted to know, after a 20-minute brief introduction to the concept of mindfulness, could people without training in meditation and mindfulness benefit?

Through brain scans, researchers evaluated the response to high heat on the forearm and reaction to a negative image. In both cases, when participants were asked to respond, as usual, the researchers found that there was a significant difference in brain signaling pathways when they asked participants to use mindfulness techniques.

Specifically, participants reported reduced negative emotions and less pain when using mindfulness techniques. These changes in the nervous system have not occurred in the prefrontal cortex, which regulates conscious or rational decision, but is the outcome of willpower consciousness. The moments of being able to tolerate pain or negative emotions, even in long-term meditation practice, offer countless clinical benefits.

HOW MINDFULNESS AFFECTS THE BRAIN

Many hospitals have introduced "mindfulness decompression" psycho-assisted treatment programs. Not only are psychiatric departments using mindfulness to help patients with depression, but also departments of brain, oncology, and gynecology, and many more.

More and more documents show that the nervous system is a modifiable network, and the changes in the adult neural structure can be achieved through training. Neuroimaging studies have begun to examine the neural mechanisms of mindfulness exercises through electroencephalography (EEG) and functional magnetic resonance imaging (MRI).

Before we proceed into the findings, we should first explore basic brain structure.

The human brain is one of the most advanced systems in nature. It is estimated that there are about 100 billion neurons in an adult's brain. These neuronal cells are connected to each other through about a quadrillion (1,000,000,000,000,000) synapses, forming a highly complex intercommunicating system. The structure of the brain network, in short, is more complex than we can imagine. The tools and media for these neurons to communicate with each other are various neurotransmitters.

So, let's look at the influence of mindfulness on brain structure and function. These aspects are important scopes for measuring the effect of mindfulness training.

- Gray matter of the brain

The gray matter of the brain is also called the cerebral cortex, which is composed of various neurons, glia and nerve fibers. The gray matter of the brain is like the "commander" of our brain. It is the center for processing information and can respond to various stimuli from the outside world. The more gray matter in the brain, the stronger the "commander" work ability. Elderly people often say, "As you get older, your brain doesn't work as well." This is because the gray matter area of the brain decreases with age. As a sidenote, it is widely accepted that Alzheimer's is a disease of the gray matter, and is perhaps an extreme example of how vital this part of the brain is to our mental competence.

- Hippocampus

The hippocampus is located between the cerebral thalamus and the medial temporal lobe. It is part of the limbic system and is mainly responsible for the storage, conversion and orientation of long-term memory. It also participates in regulating the activation of the cortex. And reaction also helps to regulate emotions.

Three parts of the brain are related to memory, namely the frontal lobe, hippocampus and diencephalon. The frontal lobe is like a USB flash drive, temporarily storing some files; the hippocampus is like a computer's hard disk, storing long-term memories. The diencephalon is used to preserve deeper memories that are rarely used.

Interestingly, often extremely elderly people can still remember things from childhood because they have entered the deep memory of the hippocampus.

Human memory declines with age because of various pressures that affect the hippocampus; studies have shown that the size of the hippocampus in patients with depression and dementia is smaller than that of healthy people.

- Amygdala

At the base of the brain, there is an almond-shaped structure called the amygdala. It is the "fear center" in the brain and is mainly responsible for regulating emotions and memory. The amygdala is related to alertness and aggressive behavior; when it is normal. For instance, if a person hears that a neighbour's dog has bitten someone, there will be a presence of fear and avoidance of the dog from then on. But if the amygdala is damaged, the fear alert and the thought of escape route in order to avoid the bite of the dog might not be there again. Anxiety, autism and Alzheimer's are all related to the loss of function of the amygdala.

Therefore, a calm amygdala allows higher cognitive functions to increase (of the prefrontal cortex or neocortex), meaning that the automatic reactions of the limbic and reptilian brains are regulated and controlled. That is, it inhibits the functions of the "old brain" that developed 120 million years ago and that today do not serve us on a daily basis, except in extreme cases.

- Default mode network

As aforementioned, the human brain is a network composed of billions of neurons, and its complexity is beyond imagination. According to the findings of many reputable scientists our brains have different so called "modes," one of which is called the default network. You may ask, what is the default? The meaning is, in reality, more comparable to "silence"; it refers to the brain network activated when the brain is in a state of rest. When the external stimulus comes and the brain has a task, the brain is activated (inhibition state).

From a biomedical point of view, the default network is a brain system, which encompasses a handful off closely connected brain areas. These areas include the posterior cingulate anterior cuneiform (PCC or Precuneus), medial prefrontal lobe (MPFC), bilateral angular gyrus, bilateral lateral temporal lobe, and bilateral hippocampus.

In our day to day lives, we are usually in the constant state of "focusing on the task at hand" or "wandering". The restful mental state is a requirement for a contented life, but is far too often left idle by us in our hectic lives filled with technology, and worries of past and future.

CHAPTER FIVE

MEDITATION

Meditation is a practice in which you gain the power of faith to create what you want by going deep into your heart to align your mind, body, and spirit. Guided meditation, deep relaxation and mind-body techniques go beyond trends, or new-age nonsense. They are researched and validated methods that have lasting benefits for radiation health, happiness and self-empowerment.

Furthermore, we can also define meditation as a family of practices that train attention to bring mental processes under greater voluntary control and cultivate specific mental qualities such as increased awareness, concentration, equanimity, and love. It aims towards the development of optimal states of consciousness and psychological well-being.

According to one definition, there are various types of meditation that lead to different meditative states, which can be seen as complementary facets leading to the achievement of comprehensive psychological well-being (Wilber, 1988). These various practices are usually divided into two broad categories: concentrative or focused attention practices and mindfulness or open monitoring practices.

In addition to providing access to altered states of consciousness, which tend to be highly pleasant, peaceful, and calm, concentrative meditation can also be applied to "dissecting ourselves, our experiences, and understanding how our conscious world is generated.

TYPES OF MEDITATION

There are different ways of meditating; some would even say that there are as many ways as there are people. However, although we cannot fathom an exact number, we can certainly identify several types of meditation.

The various methods of meditating are directly related to the purpose of the meditation. Depending on the objective, the most successful meditation will be one or the other. The various types of meditation are often associated with religious currents such as Buddhism. This religion has many forms of manifestation, which is reflected in the manifestations of meditation.

The Buddha himself recommended approaching nature for meditation: sitting on the floor or a zafu cushion in a quiet space in nature provides the ideal environment to begin meditation. In this kind of meditation, the first step is to promote a state of maximum tranquility and attention.

Although there are different types of Buddhist meditation, they all coincide in contemplative techniques, aiming to achieve high understanding and nirvana.

- Zen or Zazen meditation

Zazen is the characteristic posture used during Zen meditation. The practice of zazen does not require any goals or intentions. This posture allows one to experience a state where the mind is emptied, and parasitic thoughts and ideas no longer arise. Let's take a whistle stop tour into where zazen comes from, how to practice it, and what its benefits are.

The term zazen comes from the Japanese "za," which means "to be seated," and from the word "Zen," derived from the Chinese "chán," meaning "meditation." Zazen refers to the posture used during the practice of Zen meditation. This particular form of meditation is one of the best known throughout the world; it was born 2600 years ago, under the leadership of Shakyamuni Buddha, who established the main principles. It aims to harmonize the body, the mind, and the breath through the entire focus of attention on the posture of the body.

This kind of meditation starts from a minimalist principle that makes tranquility possible. In the rooms or classes where this type of meditation is taught, there are hardly any objects, the backgrounds are neutral, and silence reigns above all.

Posture and breathing are essential for Zen meditation. The spine must be placed straight when we sit on a chair, a cushion, or a bench. As for the legs, these are placed crossed; preferably, the hands must be one on top of the other.

Finally, we unleash relaxed and natural breathing. Zen meditation is complex to master, although it may seem very simple, as it involves total control over the body and mind.

THE BENEFITS OF ZEN MEDITATION

The benefits of zazen are similar to those of other meditation techniques. Zazen allows us in particular to:

- o Slow down the heart and lower blood pressure through its beneficial action on the autonomic nervous system.
- o Improve diaphragmatic breathing, which allows better oxygenation of the blood.
- o Improve the circulation of blood in the legs, thanks to the position of the lotus.
- o Strengthen the immune defenses.
- o Reduce stress through its relaxing action.
- o Improve cognitive abilities and reduce age-related cognitive decline (concentration, memory, attention).
- o To reduce pain, by shifting the focus to another object.

- • Transcendental meditation

Numerous studies show that transcendental meditation creates conditions for the body and mind to eliminate stress, which is often responsible for many psychological and physiological disorders. The technique primarily helps to keep the heart in good condition. It decreases the sympathetic nervous system's activity responsible for the dilation of blood vessels and reduces stress hormones (adrenaline, noradrenaline and cortisol). Studies from the American Heart Association (AHA) show that transcendental meditation dramatically reduces hypertension, atherosclerosis, narrowing blood vessels, and thickening of arteries.

TM is not related to religious beliefs, nor does it require a specific posture, state of mind, or a mantra. It is simply a subject of staying calm for a period that is generally around 20 minutes. People who successfully practice TM usually do so twice or three times a day.

- Vipassana meditation

This meditation approach is one of the oldest in India. It is considered a process of self-purification, for which a concentration is required first on the breath, later on the body, to understand the universal truths of impermanence, suffering, and the absence of ego.

Benefits of Vipassana meditation

The first beneficial effects of Vipassana meditation take place after 2 to 3 weeks of practice. Among them are:

- better concentration;
- better control of moods such as anger or hatred;
- greater wisdom;
- greater calm;
- reduced stress and anxiety;
- greater clarity of thought;
- a reduction in certain symptoms of illness or pain, both physical and psychological.

- Taoist meditation

Taoist meditation aims to use chi energy, feel it, and work with it. Often, the practice of this meditation involves feeling that energy throughout the body.

Benefits of Taoist meditation

- o It improves the blood supply to cells and promotes the elimination of toxins accumulated in the joints or muscle masses.
- o It has a toning and self-massage effect on internal organs. Its effect sometimes occurs directly under the action of the compression caused by the posture. In other cases, it is a reflex action obtained by stimulation of nerve endings. The result is an improvement in all major organ functions, thus proving to be very beneficial for all digestive problems, from liver dysfunction to diseases of the stomach and intestines. It calms the pain associated with peptic ulcers or liver engorgement and significantly improves digestion and assimilation of food.
- o It strengthens the heart by emphasizing deep breathing, unlike isometric and isotonic contractions, which tend to stress it out. The contraction phase is preceded by two preparatory phases, which aim to improve tissue oxygenation and prepare the heart and muscle masses for the effort required during the contraction phase.
- o It produces a soothing, balancing effect on the nervous system which is strongly indicated in cases of nervous diseases. Contractions prepare the body and mind for an unequaled level of relaxation; hence they are used in certain relaxation techniques. It helps hyperactive people to channel their energy. Conversely, it stimulates lymphatic people and energizes those who lack self-confidence by helping them find their way.

o It warms up and strengthens muscle masses and prepares the body before a sporting effort (certain postures, such as that of the rider or the dragon, are excellent preparation for skiing).
o It causes internal warming of tissues and accelerates cellular exchanges.
o It revitalizes and energizes the whole body. It recharges cells and improves the circulation of energy currents. Its practice quickly eliminates fatigue and provides a pleasant feeling of vitality, well-being.
o It regenerates joint areas, removes rheumatic pain, and strengthens ligaments to prevent sprains, strains, tendonitis, low back pain, sciatica, back pain.

- Guided Meditation

It is one of the more 'present' forms of meditation, and we can find an abundance in specialized centers and on social networks and platforms such as Spotify or YouTube. The main premise of guided meditation is absolutely the presence of a spiritual guide. This helps us overcome the difficulties of meditation, especially when we are beginning.

- Mindfulness meditation

This kind of modern meditation places a lot of emphasis on awareness. In a world where we carry out many activities unconsciously or without much attention, it is necessary to give value to practices that require all our concentration.

- Meditation in yoga

Many yoga practices include, begin or end with a meditation. It is a complement to any yoga practice: it helps to find a state of tranquility that is very beneficial for the practice of asanas.

There are countless forms and sub-forms of meditation if we consider the traditional and more modern interpretations. It is essential for us to choose well which are best suited to us, since depending on our physical and mental activity we will need one class or another.

ELEMENTS OF MEDITATION

The various types of meditation comprise of different elements to help you meditate. These can vary depending on who guides the students or who teaches the class. Some of the most frequent elements in meditation include:

- Focus attention: Concentrating attention is generally one of the most important elements of meditation; it is what helps free your mind from the many distractions that cause stress and worry. You can focus your attention on things like a specific object, an image, a mantra, or even a breath.
- Relaxed breathing: This approach involves deep, even breathing, using the diaphragm muscle to expand the lungs. The purpose is to slow down your breathing, receive more oxygen, and reduce the use of the muscles in your shoulders, neck, and upper chest when breathing, in order to breathe more efficiently.

- A peaceful place: If you are a beginner, practicing meditation will be easier if you are in a quiet place with few distractions, including no television, radio, or mobile phone, which you may find hard to escape in today's world. With more experience in meditation, you may eventually be able to meditate anywhere, even in high-stress situations when you will benefit the most from meditating, such as in a traffic jam, in a stressful work meeting, or waiting in a long line at the airport or supermarket.
- A comfortable position: You can practice meditation sitting, walking, lying down, during activities or in other positions. Just try to be relaxed so you can get the most out of your meditation. Try to maintain good posture throughout.
- Open attitude: Allow thoughts to pass through your mind without judgment.

MINDFULNESS MEDITATION AND ITS USE IN THERAPEUTIC CONTEXTS

The vast development of meditative strategies by the Buddhist tradition to diminish human suffering, and in particular the practice of "mindfulness", has steadily penetrated Western culture during the course of the 20th century, and its adaptation with therapeutic purposes has found fertile ground in behavioral medicine, health psychology and cognitive therapy (Kabat-Zinn, 1990, 2003; Miró 2006b). Such areas of health are characterized by stating that mental and emotional factors, the way we think and behave, can have important effects on our physical and mental health when we are healthy, and on our ability to recover or improve our quality of life when we are physically or mentally ill.

Consequently, the mindfulness approach has demonstrated, through over twenty-five years of progressively more abundant and complex research, its effectiveness in areas as diverse as the prevention of depressive relapses (Segal, Teasdale & Williams, 2002); reducing stress and increasing quality of life in cancer patients (Carlson, Speca, Patel & Goodey, 2003; Speca, Carlson, Goodey & Angen, 2000); chronic pain relief and fibromyalgia (Kabat-Zinn, 1982; Kabat-Zinn, Lipworth, and Burney, 1985; Kabat-Zinn, Lipworth, Burney, and Sellers, 1987; Kaplan, Goldenberg, and Galvin, 1993; Goldenberg, Kaplan, Nadeau, Brodeur, Smith and Schmid, 1994); and the recovery of skin tissues in patients with psoriasis (Kabat-Zinn, Wheeler, Light, Skillings, Scharf and Cropley 1998; Kabat-Zinn, 2003), among others.

The fact that mindfulness, although coming from a contemplative tradition, is essentially a skill that can be trained and that its teaching and practice can be done independently of any type of religious affiliation or belief, makes it especially suitable for implementation in contexts therapies through practice groups led by qualified instructors. In this sense, the contextualization of this therapeutic intervention as training in skills empowers the user of the health system, returning responsibility for the improvement of their quality of life, and taking them from a passive-receptive position of "patient" to an active- person responsible, which in itself is a significant paradigm shift in the context of a semi-rural public hospital in particular, and in any health context that seeks to approach a comprehensive view, in general.

At present, there are various psychotherapeutic approaches based on mindfulness that are already part of the mainstream of contemporary psychology, gradually leaving the terrain of the alternative or complementary. This professionalisation of the applications of mindfulness in health and the interest it is receiving from the scientific society is also reflected in the wide proliferation of publications on the subject in journals indexed with a peer review system. Among the therapeutic approaches based on mindfulness, those that currently have the most empirical support are the stress program reduction based on mindfulness (MBSR: Kabat-Zinn, 1990, 2003); mindfulness-based cognitive therapy (MBCT: Segal Teasdale and Williams, 2002); acceptance and commitment therapy (ACT: Hayes, Strosahl & Houts, 2005) and dialectical behavioral therapy (DBT: Linehan, 1993), used in the treatment of borderline personality disorder and decreased suicidal behavior.

In these therapeutic models, the practice of mindfulness is taught through variations and developments of the program initially proposed by Kabat-Zinn at the Stress Reduction Clinic of the University of Massachusetts School of Medicine. This program is currently offered in more than 250 hospitals and clinics in different parts of the world. There is no evidence that it had been previously applied in any hospital in Chile until this pilot experience. It is encouraging to mention that at the time of submitting this article for publication, there are currently at least two other clinical teams implementing the mindfulness-based stress.

MINDFULNESS BASED STRESS REDUCTION PROGRAM

The REBAP program carried out at the Santa Bárbara Hospital closely follows the guidelines and practices of the original model by Kabat-Zinn (1990), although enriched by the contributions of the manual developed by Segal, Teasdale and Williams (2002) in their program prevention of depressive relapses through the practice of mindfulness. The Segal, Teasdale, and Williams model which already enjoys great respectability for its efficacy (Miró, 2006a), resembles conventional cognitive therapy in its emphasis on awareness of depressogenic ruminative cognitive patterns. The difference is that its objective is not the change from "mental contents" to other more positive or objective ones, but the change in the type of relationship that the person has with their own thoughts.

Through the practice of mindfulness, both in formal instances and in everyday life, the practitioner becomes progressively able to recognize and observe his thoughts instead of taking them as if they were indisputable facts, gradually misidentifying themself from their mental contents and associated conflict emotions, thus being able to evaluate each circumstance experienced more fully and being able to respond creatively and effectively, instead of reacting automatically from their usual patterns (Segal, Teasdale & Williams, 2002).

This program, which was offered as a stress-reduction workshop for Hospital workers and patients, consisted of 8 weekly group sessions of 2 and a half hours each, space in which various practices were taught experientially to develop mindfulness. These practices can be divided into formal and informal practices. Among the first are:

a) The "body scan", a 40-minute exercise in which attention is directed sequentially to each part of the body while the person is lying on their back with their eyes closed.

b) "Sitting meditation", where participants are instructed to sit in a relaxed and alert posture by directing their attention to the sensations of breathing.

c) The "hatha yoga," a practice of bringing mindfulness to bodily sensations during gentle stretches while standing and lying down. Within informal practices, participants are instructed to carry out daily activities outside the sessions such as eating, brushing teeth or walking, in an attitude of presence and attention towards the present experience.

For each practice, formal or informal, the participants are instructed to focus their attention on a specific aspect such as the feet when walking or the abdomen's movement when breathing - observing with equanimity the expected emergence of various thoughts, emotions or sensations. When the person notices that they have been distracted and that their mind has wandered towards other thoughts, fantasies or memories, the practice consists of recognizing the content of that thought at that moment and returning to the focus of attention. This circular process of a) paying mindfulness, b) becoming distracted, and c) noticing that one has become distracted and kindly returning to mindfulness, can take place literally hundreds of times during the first few practice sessions.

Along with formal and informal practices, during the weekly group session, various aspects of stress are discussed, such as mind-body interaction, the fight-flight response, or relational stress, and a wide range of topics are discussed, and ways to cope with stress using mindfulness tools that are gradually learned in the program shared. An example of this is the exercise consisting of mindful breathing for three minutes three times a day, at times predefined by the person. In this practice, the person stops the activity they are doing, straightens their spine - they can stand or sit - and turns their attention to the movement of their abdomen during inhalation and exhalation.

An important aspect of the program is to complement the work during the sessions, with at least half an hour a day of formal practice - body scan, yoga, meditation - using CDs with the audio instructions of the exercises during the first weeks, in addition to the performance of informal practices and recording in protocols delivered week by week by the instructor together with the summary of the central points of each session. The high level of commitment and perseverance required by the program is one of its distinctive qualities (Segal, Tasdale & Williams, 2002; Kabat-Zinn, 1990).

STUDIES ON THE BENEFITS OF MEDITATION

Looking to more specific studies, a team of neurologists from the Waisman Center of the University of Wisconsin, United States, in collaboration with the Scheche Monastery, Kathmandu, Nepal, studied the brains of a group of young Buddhist monk disciples from the schools Nyingmapa and Kagyupa meditation studies, and compared them to those of American college students.

The results of the encephalograms and other tests on both groups revealed that the number of neuronal connections of the monks was notably higher than that of the university students. In other words, they had a more active brain. Also, in collaboration with Yale University and MIT, a study by the Massachusetts General Hospital measured different aspects of the brain of a group of individuals who practiced mindfulness for thirty minutes a day for eight weeks, compared to a control group who did not meditate.

The results were a greater thickness and density of gray matter in the hippocampus, the area of the brain related to learning, concentration, empathy and memory, and a reduction in the size of the brain amygdala, the area related to stress and anxiety. In the control group, by contrast, these changes had not occurred.

Another 2009 study reported significant improvements in patients with coronary heart disease from continued meditation practice. The New York Times also echoed in 2007 another study that claimed that people who meditated improved their ability to concentrate in the long term; that is, they could stay focused longer on an activity without feeling tired or distracted.

Along the same lines, another 2008 study published in the journal PloS One showed that practitioners of meditation had a greater capacity to capture resonances from people who suffered, and experienced feelings of compassion with more intensity than people who did not meditate. Finally, a study in which scientists from Spain, France, and the United States participated showed how meditation inhibited the expression of genes related to inflammatory processes and pain, which can have a positive impact on the risk of suffering from diseases like cancer, as in the formation of arterial atheromas.

THE BENEFITS OF MEDITATION ACCORDING TO SCIENCE

Science defines meditation as a habit carried out daily for long periods of time bringing multiple benefits to those who practice it. Indeed, there is plentiful scientific and journalistic literature on the benefits to people who practice some of the very varied forms of meditation that exist, be it conscious and slow breathing for a period of time, the practice of elementary mindfulness, the simple silent contemplation of nature, walks through the forest, or the most elaborate Buddhist disciplines of Asian origin.

One study reveals that the expression of the precursor genes of inflammatory and pain processes, that is, of the secretion of cortisol and other compounds responsible for inflammation, can be reduced or even blocked by the continued practice of meditation. In other words, through it, we can control the expression of certain blocks of our genome.

Additionally, other studies speak of an improvement in cardiovascular health in people who practice meditation, as well as a reduction in stress levels, both more predictable and logical benefits if we take into account that meditation involves stopping, regaining control over our rhythm respiratory -and therefore cardiac stability- and disconnect from the noise of anguish and problems that surround us. In any case, all these benefits are observed after long periods of constant practice and not due to the sporadic and short-lived exercise of meditation.

CHAPTER SIX

GUIDED MEDITATION

Almost all human beings live in the fast lane of a fast-changing world, and operates consistently as we strive to keep up with ever developing technology. Every day, we face huge challenges in finance, family, career and interpersonal relationships. These challenges are exhausting; keeping up with this busy rhythm generates a high degree of anxiety and pressure in the most laid back of people. With high anxiety and stress, we become inferior, out of touch, sometimes numb, and lose control, while our self-esteem plummets to new lows. Connecting with our interior becomes necessary in these situations, and meditation is an unrivaled way to achieve it. However, meditating is not an easy task, and therefore it is essential to turn to expert teachings to guide us. So, without further ado, lets delve into what guided meditation is, what benefits it entails, and what variances there are within this class of meditation.

Guided meditation is a tool that allows, through words and images, to put aside negative emotions such as pain, stress, and day-to-day worries, helping us to connect with our interior.

This technique has become increasingly popular. On the one hand, due to the need to manage the stress of today's society and, on the other, because it is an easily applicable tool on a day-to-day basis.

The way guided meditation is done is quite simple. A person who operates as an expert in meditation, such as a guru or spiritual guide, offers a series of instructions to one reach a state of relaxation.

With their expert knowledge, the conductor helps to focus on the personal goals of the person who comes to them. These goals can be an improved emotional state in general, accepting a situation in which there is no control, or psychological preparation towards a specific objective. It is for this reason that it is widely used in the training of elite athletes.

To carry it out, you can attend specialized workshops and gyms, but our ever developing technological world, which we may strive to distance ourselves from, also offers the prospect of practicing from home; especially considering there is, fortunately, no need for copious space or resources to meditate.

TYPES OF GUIDED MEDITATION

There are several reasons why guided meditation is used; we each have differing goals. That is why we see variances within the principal subject, used according to the problem of those who require it:

- Traditional meditations

The spiritual guide or guru gives the instructions orally, guiding the listener into a meditative state. There are usually numerous pauses of silence, and it is common that these will be accompanied with music.

The purpose of this type of meditation can be varied, but it is usually used to start or to maintain a state of calm.

- Meditation with visualization

You are invited to imagine an object or scene to achieve greater relaxation. Recurring resources are the rays of light of different colors, each representing an emotion with which one is going to work.

- Relaxation and body scan

The purpose of the 'body scan' is to achieve the maximum degree of relaxation at the body level. The person becomes aware of all parts of his body and even his body temperature.

They are usually accompanied by music or relaxing sounds of nature, directing those guided into a state of deep calm.

- Binaural tones

According to physicist Heinrich Wilhelm Dove, by presenting two sounds with different frequencies in each ear, the mind tries to reconcile the difference by creating a third wave. Headphones are placed on, and audio is presented in which a different sound is presented on each side.

According to the followers of this type of guided meditation, using binaural tones stimulates alpha waves and connects with the body's interior part.

- Affirmations

Instead of thinking negatively, this branch of guided meditation proposes to reformulate these thoughts in a more optimistic format: "I'm in good health," "I've come very far."

- Guided mindfulness meditation

We breathe all our lives, non-stop, and yet we do not pay enough attention to this natural process.

The premise behind this type of guided meditation is that if you can control something as simple and fundamental as your breath, you can build from this foundation to train your mind in almost any aspect.

- Guided meditations for better sleep

This is one of the most commonplace sub-forms of guided meditation, given that we live in a society in which schedules prevent us from having adequate sleep habits.

Most people have trouble sleeping at some point in their life. In fact, some struggle with the debilitating inability to drift seamlessly into sleep for much of their life. Often, when we go to bed, we start to calculate how much time they have before having to get up to go to work, or school, or even to do the things we enjoy; this is where a sense of panic starts to arise. Our problem is that the more you want to sleep, the more difficult it is to achieve.

Guided meditations for better sleep offer a series of instructions that help achieve sleep naturally and voluntarily.

While trying to sleep, we tend to review what has happened throughout the day, but through guided meditation we can detect negative emotions and gradually put them aside.

HOW GUIDED MEDITATION WORKS

With guided meditation, you don't need to know how to meditate. All you need is your ability to listen, and you will effortlessly enter the waters of subconscious renewal. The subconscious controls 37.2 trillion cells in your body and regulates and connects all 12 systems that enable you to survive and function, including cardiovascular, endocrine glands, respiratory system, nervous system, immune system, circulatory system, digestion system, lymphatic system, muscle, bone, reproductive and urinary system. This simple guidance into a meditative state allows the most inexperienced of us to take control of our subconscious.

Guided meditation is childishly simple and allows beginners to commence meditative practice easily. You do not have to worry about making a mistake, and do not have to question your technique, since it suffices to listen to the instructions. Just follow them. Guided meditation invites you to apply simple principles to discover what it is to meditate. It is the verbalization of what you will have to learn to do without thinking about reaching a higher stage of concentration.

At first, guided meditation is there to prevent you from thinking about the process itself. Then, when you have practiced enough to do without the meditation guide, you can begin the more fulfilling practice of meditating on your own, without guidance. That way, the instructions won't clutter your mind. The meditation guide's role is hence to be a reminder; a map to help you refrain from worrying about where to go, how to get there.

Often, guided meditation will be in the form of an audio file or a video with a voice giving you simple instructions. You do not need any prior knowledge of meditation to follow them since they encompass all known concepts. From these, you will endeavor to improve your perception and deepen your focus. The voice clearly tells you what to do, whilst you remain completely involved in your meditation session. If images are present, they will, every so often, help you to detach yourself from the more mundane sensations; it will allow you to work more in depth with yourself and go beyond the most obvious aspects of meditation.

REASONS FOR GUIDED MEDITATION

Meditating with the benefit of a guide allows you to practice initially without worrying about prior knowledge. You don't have to be afraid of doing wrong. You also do not have to discover abstract concepts that are sometimes difficult to grasp for those who have never meditate.

Verbal guidance allows us to take our first steps in a new world and favor direct experience over book learning. You benefit from first-hand knowledge; you refine your perception and your sensations. Finally, you learn to focus more deeply because you can break free from the protocol that is supported by the file.

Guided meditation is not a meditation of lesser quality; it is simply an accompaniment to take your first steps. It is learning to walk before learning to run. We will ultimately 'run' when we have unlocked enough concepts and learned enough about ourselves to know where to go. You will know where to go and how to get there. Guided meditation is nothing more than a way to meditate immediately rather than getting lost in misunderstanding.

HORMONAL AND CELLULAR FUNCTIONS OF MEDITATION

Both guided meditation and deep relaxation have many amazing effects on your body and hormones.

- Meditation slows down brain wave activity and relieves stress while triggering human growth hormone (HGH). HGH helps regulate metabolism, stimulates fat cells to reduce the amount of stored fat, promotes protein synthesis in cells, and plays a role in regulating blood sugar.
- Meditation helps to calm the adrenal glands and rest them, freeing them from excessive production of cortisol (stress hormone), which can have a devastating effect on your thyroid function and weight loss.
- Meditation will remove your endocrine system from a high alert state. Hormone secretion is regulated, and all your hormonal systems (thyroid, adrenal glands, sex hormones, etc.) have the opportunity to restore balance.
- Both meditation and deep relaxation can make your body justly rest. This is when you restore balance and rejuvenate your entire body. The same also applies to their effect our ability to experience quality sleep. Meditation helps to

eliminate endless mental chat and, in doing so, improve the eminence of sleep.

- Meditation alkalises your system and balances the acidity of fear thoughts that are caused by your overactive analytical thinking and the production of stress hormones.
- Meditation can reduce inflammation at the cellular level, neutralize acidosis and minimize pain.

FURTHER PRACTTICAL MEDITATION METHODOLOGY

Breathing methods: chest breathing, abdominal breathing, and full breathing are the most common breathing methods in yoga. Meditation methodology varies widely in its complexity, but often the simplest approaches are the most effective:

- *Counting method:* Focus on breathing, counting between natural exhales and breaths, counting from 1 to 5, from 1 to 10, and repeating. You will find that you count more and more unconsciously, and returning to 1, rather that continuing ceaselessly, is a very good reminder of what we are aiming to gain from the exercise.
- *Body scan:* Use consciousness of the body's form to relax, as a whole, from feet, legs, hips, back to head; stretch your eyebrows, relax clenched teeth, let your shoulder blades fall flat etc.
- *Voice meditation:* The yoga voice is called Mantra and consists of Sanskrit syllables. For example, our most commonly used OM chanting.

o *Blueprint meditation:* a spiritual guide to imagine images. Use your mind's eye to organise the blueprint in your cognizance and find a sense of inner peace. For example, the singing of birds and the fragrance of flowers, the blue sky and white clouds, the stream of water, and so on.

o *Candlelight meditation:* This is a typical meditation of observing external objects, gazing at the candlelight, focusing on observing its inner flame, outer flame, color, size, and shape. Try not to blink your eyes and let the tears flow naturally without judgement.

o *Music meditation:* put simply, listen to your preferred light music to enter meditation.

GUIDED MEDITATION: AS EFFECTIVE AS CLINICAL THERAPY?

Decades of research shows us that the best way to get the mind out of this inner spin and promote sleep is to incorporate a regular mindfulness habit.

UCLA researchers have found that mindfulness is as effective when working with sleep as clinical therapy or sleeping pills, and of course, without side effects.

The rational is that the practice of mindfulness allows us to reach an optimal point of nervous balance during the day so that by nightfall, the body and mind are ready to initiate a deep and restful sleep.

But there are many other reasons meditation has this effect. Research from the HeartMath Institute has revealed that when we are over-stimulated, overwhelmed, stressed, or worried, our breathing becomes accelerated and shallow, with which our pattern of heart variability becomes irregular and our nervous system receives alarm signals. Rapid breathing closes the door to the realm of dreams.

The practice of mindfulness by pausing our respiratory rhythm and using the diaphragm sends safety signals to the nervous system, with which we quickly get out of threat mode. We activate a relaxation response, the mind lets go of all that maelstrom of negativity, and we are ready for a deep night's sleep. The nervous system understands that everything is fine and there is no more need to protect itself.

And the most interesting thing is that you do not need to do your mindfulness practice at night. You can choose to do the practice at any other time of the day. For example, even if you practice in the morning, you will notice that you can sleep more peacefully when you go to bed.

Before going to sleep, it is also advisable to invoke positive thoughts. Researchers at the Faculty of Psychology at the University of Manchester, England, discovered that people who feel grateful and positive before going to bed sleep longer and report greater rest than people who maintain a mental chatter where negative thoughts dominate. If you have trouble bringing up positive thoughts, try writing in a Gratitude Journal before bed.

In addition to practicing mindfulness, creating a space of silence and stillness is also essential. Noise causes great disturbances in our brain. At any din, the sound waves vibrate in the bones of the ear, transmitting the movement to the cochlea (the snail-shaped area), which converts physical vibrations into electrical signals that are received by the brain. The body reacts immediately (and strongly) to these signals, even in the middle of deep sleep. Neurophysiological research suggests that the noises cause an immediate release of stress hormones like cortisol.

Furthermore, the physical effects of noise are cumulative, negatively affecting our cognitive abilities (mainly attention, memory, and problem solving) and decreasing our motivation. Silence appears to have the opposite effect of noise on our brain. While noise can activate the biological mechanisms of stress and anxiety, silence releases tension in the brain and body; through neurogenesis, it is able to regenerate what excess noise made us lose. In one study, Luciano Bernardi and his colleagues found that two minutes of silence can be even more relaxing than listening to 'soothing ' music.

Duke University regenerative biologist Imke Kirste found that two hours of silence per day boosted cell development in the hippocampus. This neurogenesis or growth of new cells in the brain has opened the door to the development of therapeutic strategies based on silence.

TV, computers, and smartphones before bed is a bad idea, and it is vital to avoid contact with artificial light sources before going to bed if our goal remains to achieve superior sleep.

Light suppresses the production of melatonin, the so-called sleep hormone. And this includes e-book readers, telephones, televisions, laptops, or any other type of screen.

Before going to bed, it is advisable to avoid exposure to any type of light. Bright lights - including blue light coming from electronic devices - can trick the brain into registering it as daylight, causing sleep cycles to become unbalanced.

It is also important to pay attention to the transition time between the waking state and sleep. Many experts recommend creating a small routine that predisposes us to sleep.

One useful technique is to set an alarm an hour before going to bed. When the alarm goes off, we turn off all the lights, unplug the screens, and begin our guided, or unguided, meditation.

Don't try so hard in order to get to sleep. A tremendously common but often overlooked cause of insomnia is putting too much effort into getting to sleep.

In his Dreamland: Adventures in the Strange Science of Sleep, author David K. Randall argues that the more urgent and necessary sleep is, the more elusive it becomes. The studies compiled by the author show that if we force ourselves into falling asleep, it takes us longer to do so: when our minds stay focused on inducing sleep, our psychic resources begin to perform a progress check, which opens the door to all kinds of musings and mental detours that prevent us from entering into the land of dreams. Worst of all, if we experience this problem every night, we can create a state of chronic insomnia.

At bedtime, victory is in surrender. Thinking about it is the last thing we should do. We need to face our rest by creating an inner state of stillness and calm. Thinking and thinking that we should sleep only makes the process more difficult. Mindfulness helps you with this by sending safety signals to the nervous system; you enter an inner state of serenity that allows you to stop worrying compulsively and let yourself go. You come out of the mental effort, and you settle in the presence. The practice of mindfulness is so effective for sleep because it brings together all the factors that the body needs: it installs us in stillness and silence, uses slow and deep breathing, avoids eye contact with artificial light, and sends signals of calm to the nervous system. Mindfulness is a perfect technique to promote deep and restful sleep, and practicing can be as simple as sitting in a chair for 20 minutes a day.

STRESS MANAGEMENT

We all feel tensed at some point or another. It is a normal and healthy reaction to a change or challenge. But stress that continues for more than a few weeks can affect your health. Prevent stress from making you sick by learning healthy ways to deal with it.

The first measure that can be taken in managing stress is recognizing the presence of stress in your life. Everyone experiences stress differently. You may be angry or irritable, unable to sleep or have headaches or an upset stomach. Once you know the signs to look for, you can start driving it away.

Secondly, identify situations that cause the stress. Your stressors can be family, work, school, money, health problems, or relationships. As soon as you know where your stress is coming from, you can identify ways to deal with your stressors.

FINDING HEALTHY TECHNIQUES TO MANAGE STRESS

There are many ways to manage stress. It is recommended to practice several before concluding which ones work best for you.

Recognize the things you cannot change: Accepting that you cannot change certain things allows you to let them go and not remain upset. For example, you cannot change the fact that you must drive during rush hour. But you can find ways to relax on the go, like listening to a podcast or an audiobook.

Avoid stressful situations: Whenever possible, stay away from the source of stress. For example, if your family argues more often during the holidays, give yourself a break and go for a walk or a drive.

Workout: Being physically agile every day is the best and easiest way to deal with stress. When you do exercise, your brain releases chemicals that make you feel good. It can also help you with your pent up energy or frustration. Find something you enjoy, whether it's walking, biking, playing football, skateboarding, fishing, swimming, or dancing, and do it for at least 30 minutes on most days.

Change your perspective: Try to develop a more positive attitude concerning challenges. You can do this by substituting negative thoughts with more positive thoughts. For example, instead of thinking, "why does everything always go wrong?" Change that idea to, "I can find a way to overcome this." It may seem difficult or silly at first, but you will find that this helps you turn your perspective around.

Do something you enjoy: When stress takes you down, do something you enjoy to help get you back on your feet. It can be something that is as simple as reading a good book, listening to music, watching your favorite movie, or going out to dinner with a friend. Or start a new hobby or class. No matter what you choose, try to do at least one thing a day that is just for you.

Learn new ways to relax: Practicing relaxation approaches is a great way to deal with day-to-day stress. Relaxation techniques help lower your heart rate and lower your blood pressure. There are many types, from deep breaths and meditation, to yoga and tai chi. Take a class or try to learn from books, videos, or online resources.

Connect with your loved ones: Don't allow stress get between you and your social life. Spending time with family and friends can also help you feel better and forget about stress. Entrusting your problems to a friend will, more often than not, help you solve them.

Get enough sleep: Getting enough rest at night can help you think more clearly and have more energy. Perhaps this is more difficult than it sounds, but as we have already seen there are foolproof ways of achieving this goal. Sufficient sleep will also make it easier to handle any issues that may arise in your day to day life. Try to get 7-9 hours of sleep each night.

Eat a healthy diet: Eating healthy foods helps fuel your body and mind. Avoid snacks that are high in sugar and eat plenty of vegetables, fruits, whole grains, reduced or fat-free dairy, and lean protein.

Learn to say no: If your stress comes from doing too many tasks at home or work, learn to set limits it and ask others for help when you need it.

Avoiding relieving stress in unhealthy ways

When feeling stressed, you can resort to unhealthy behaviors to help you relax. These behaviors can include:

- Eat excessively
- Smoking cigarettes
- Drinking alcohol and using drugs
- Not sleeping enough or sleeping too much

All these may help you feel better in the short term, but they are likely to hurt you more than they help in the long term. Instead, find healthy ways to reduce stress; as we have recognised, these are abundant.

CHAPTER SEVEN

ANXIETY

Anxiety is the emotional reflection of people's serious deterioration of the valued characteristics of reality or future things. The opposite form of emotion is anticipation; that is, anticipation is the emotional reflection of a person's apparent positive trend towards the valued characteristics of reality or future things.

Anxiety itself is a normal emotional reflection of human beings, but excessive or weak anxiety will form emotional or physiological diseases. For example, being insensitive to the country in a period of crisis without worrying about the country and the people is a typical emotional or physiological disease. Conversely, and more commonplace, excessive anxiety caused by small changes in personal interests or generated for no coherent reason is also an emotional or physiological disease.

An anxiety attack, without being a serious event for health, generates a panic situation that causes symptoms very similar to those of a heart attack, to the point that it can be confused as so. It occurs instantly, without warning, and reaches its maximum intensity in a matter of very few minutes, and can last for what feels like hours.

STRESS AND ANXIETY DISORDERS

Both stress and anxiety are natural responses of the body to the perception of imminent or future danger. Thanks to these responses, the body is activated and prepares itself to deal with these stimuli. Although they are adaptive responses, they can become a problem when the duration, frequency, and intensity are excessive or disproportionate to the stimulus that causes them. These alert and activation responses that they cause in the body are incompatible with falling asleep. For this reason, they require intervention when they are prolonged since they usually cause psychophysiological sleep problems. Anxiety and stress are one of the first precipitators of transient sleep problems.

These feelings may cause physical symptoms such as tachycardia or a tremor. Some common anxiety disorders are generalized anxiety disorder, specific phobia, social anxiety disorder, separation anxiety disorder, agoraphobia, panic disorder, and selective mutism. Anxiety disorders are distinguished by the cause of the symptoms and it is common for people to have more than one anxiety disorder.

Both heredity and environment may be the cause of anxiety. Child abuse, family history of mental illness, and poverty may all be risk factors for anxiety. Anxiety disorders often happen together with other mental illnesses, such as major depressive disorder, personality abnormalities or addictions. It takes at least six months of clinical observation to diagnose anxiety disorders properly. Excessive anxiety affects a normal lifestyle. In addition, hyperthyroidism, heart disease, use of caffeine, addiction to alcohol, the abuse of cannabis or certain drugs can all have similar symptoms of anxiety.

Anxiety disorder usually does not recover on its own without treatment. Treatment methods include changing lifestyles, seeking counseling, and medication control, as well as, increasingly, the use of mindfulness and meditation. Counseling usually cooperates with cognitive behavioral therapy for treatment. Medications that can improve symptoms include antidepressants and anxiolytics (such as benzodiazepines, β-receptor blockers and buspirone).

CAUSES OF AN ANXIETY ATTACK

There are known physical problems that can trigger (hyperthyroidism, consumption of alcohol or drugs, etc.). Still, the most common is that these types of episodes are associated with the causes of a psychological nature, such as stress. We must also bear in mind that the anxiety attack can be a symptom of a mental disorder, such as agoraphobia, social phobia, and other types of phobias.

However, an 'anxiety crisis' should not be confused with what is known in psychiatry as a generalized anxiety disorder. While in this case, the person is permanently ill or on a recurring basis, those who suffer from an anxiety crisis are perfectly fine before it occurs, and between one problem and another.

CLASSIFICATION OF ANXIETY

- Realistic anxiety

Unlike pathological anxiety, reality anxiety is an emotional response to the potential challenges or threats of reality. This emotional response is adapted to the facts of real threats and is something a person cannot control when facing the general reaction to an event situation. Characteristically, the intensity of anxiety is consistent with the degree of a real threat and disappears with the real threat's disappearance; it has adaptive significance.

It helps individuals to mobilize the body's potential and resources to deal with real threats and gradually achieve the sense of control and effective problem-solving measures needed to deal with challenges until this real threat is controlled or eliminated. Therefore, realistic anxiety is the basic emotional response of human beings to adapt and solve problems. It is an emotional and behavioral response method that human beings form in the process of evolution to adapt to and respond to the environment.

- Pathological anxiety

Pathological anxiety refers to the continuous feeling of nervousness without specific reasons, or the sense of disaster, threat of imminent disaster that has no basis in reality, accompanied by obvious autonomic dysfunction and motor anxiety, often accompanied by subjective pain or Social function being impaired.

The above concept includes the following basic characteristics:

- The intensity of anxiety has no realistic basis or is obviously not commensurate with the threat of reality
- Anxiety leads to mental pain and a decrease in self-efficacy
- Anxiety is relatively long-lasting, it does not disappear with the resolution of objective problems, and is often related to personality characteristics
- A tense emotional state characterized by autonomic nervous system symptoms, including

chest discomfort, palpitations, shortness of breath, etc.

- Foreseeing disaster or misfortune, experiencing unusual pain and fear of the pre-perceived threats and lack of ability to cope, and even the actual adaptation is affected.

TYPES OF ANXIETY DISORDER

- Generalized anxiety disorder

People with generalized anxiety disorder encounter excessive anxiety or worry on most days for at least six months in a row. They may feel restless, nervous, and may tire easily. They may also have trouble concentrating, irritability, muscle tension and trouble sleeping.

People suffering from this disease often experience unspecified but persistent fears and worries, and worry excessively about countless things, real or imagined, in their daily lives. Its specific manifestation is a chronic excessive worry. The following symptoms appear: weakness, inattention, irritability, muscle tension, sleep problems. Generalized anxiety disorder is the most common anxiety disorder to affect older adults and is commonly a symptom of drug abuse; medical experts pay explicit attention to this. A person can be diagnosed as a GAD patient only if he is overly worried about daily problems for six months or more. Some patients may have problems with daily decision-making and memory because excessive anxiety reduces their concentration. They appear to be strained with sweating in the hands, feet, and armpits, which are often accompanied by signs of depression after lengthy struggles with GAD. Before the diagnosis of anxiety disorder, the physician must rule out anxiety caused solely by drug intake.

GAD in children may be accompanied by symptoms such as headache, irritability, abdominal pain, and palpitations, being most typical at the age of eight to nine.

- Panic disorder

This causes panic attacks; that is, sudden feelings of terror even when there is no real danger. Physical symptoms include a rapid heartbeat, chest or stomach pain, and shortness of breath. One may also feel weak or dizzy, sweaty and experience chills, or numb hands. It is not uncommon for the sufferer to believe that they are experiencing a heart attack. Interestingly, panic disorder is more common in women than in men.

Panic disorder patients often experience intense fear and anxiety in a short period of time, causing tremors, cognitive confusion, dizziness, nausea, and/or breathing difficulties. The American Psychiatric Association (APA) defines these panics as sharp fear and anxiety that occur in a period of fewer than ten minutes, but which can last for several hours. The fuse of these symptoms may be stress, irrational thinking, general fear, fear of the unknown, or even exercise. However, sometimes the fuse is unknown, and these symptoms may appear without warning. Patients can prevent symptoms by avoiding this fuse, but far too often it is not that simple to intervene.

In addition to repeated panic attacks, panic disorder diagnosis requires that the aforementioned episodes have chronic consequences: worry about the potential impact of symptoms, continued worry about future episodes, or major changes in behavior related to the episode. In essence, those with panic disorder will experience symptoms even in addition to the more specific panic attacks. Many with panic disorder will notice normal changes in their heartbeat, leading them to think that they have a heart problem or are about to have another panic attack. In some cases, there is an excessive increase in awareness of bodily functions during a panic attack (known as hypervigilance), where any perceived physiological changes are interpreted as potentially life-threatening diseases (i.e., extreme hypochondriasis).

- Obsessive-compulsive disorder (OCD)

OCD causes frequent and disturbing obsessions or compulsions. It causes an overwhelming urge to repeat certain behaviors. Common obsessions include fear of dirt or germs, fear of hurting yourself or wanting to fix things in a certain way. The person tends to cling to these obsessions and may have thoughts and rituals that interfere with daily life. For example, if you fear your home will be burglarized, you may repeatedly lock the door and be afraid to leave. Fascinatingly, this disorder is almost always hereditary.

- Special Phobia

A phobia is an intense fear or aversion to specific situations or objects. This fear is exaggerated with respect to the danger of the situation or the object.

People with phobias feel irrational worry and take steps to avoid the alleged danger. They may also experience immediate anxiety upon encountering the situation or object they fear. Some common phobias are flying in an airoplane, heights, animals or injections.

- Agoraphobia

Agoraphobia refers to a specific type of anxiety that involves feeling anxious about getting away from a difficult or embarrassing place or where help is ineffective. Agoraphobia and panic disorder are closely related and are often accompanied by fear of panic attacks. Common manifestations include the need to be particularly sensitive to doors or other escape routes. The term Agoraphobia is often used to refer to the avoidance behavior that patients often develop. These avoidance behaviors frequently have serious consequences in themselves, and often lead to worsening fear.

- Social phobia

Social phobia, also known as social disorder, refers to the specific fear of public situations, and of seeking to avoid public censorship or scrutiny, public embarrassment, humiliation, or social interaction. This fear can occur in specific situations (for example, during public speeches), or more typically, in all social situations. Social anxiety usually manifests through specific symptoms of weakness, such as sweating and stuttering. Along with all fear disorders, those with social disorders will try to avoid their anxiety and develop avoidance behaviors, which may cause problems and even lead to social isolation.

Social physique anxiety (SPA) is a subcategory of social anxiety. SPA is common in adolescence, especially in women.

- Separation anxiety disorder

This refers to a feeling of excessive and inappropriate anxiety caused by separation from a particular person or place. Separation anxiety is a normal part of infants or children, but only when this anxiety reaches excessive levels can it be considered a disorder. Separation anxiety disorder affects approximately 7% of adults and 4% of children, but children's cases are usually more severe; in some cases, even a small separation can cause panic, and treating children early can prevent later problems. Treatment includes training parents and family members on how to deal with the problem. Often, parents will worsen anxiety because they do not know how to deal with separation anxiety disorder with their children correctly. In addition to parent therapy, there are also medications such as SSRI that can also be used to treat separation anxiety.

- Situational anxiety

Situational anxiety is caused by new situations or changes in things. It can also be caused by existing events that make the individual uncomfortable. This anxiety is extremely common. Some situations may cause panic and anxiety in people, but will not in others. Each major event in life, such as entering university, getting married or having children can cause situational anxiety.

- Post-traumatic stress disorder (PTSD)

PTSC affects people who have experienced or witnessed a traumatic event such as a war, a natural catastrophe, a serious accident, or physical or sexual abuse. It can cause involuntary and disturbing memories of the event, difficulty sleeping, nightmares, feelings of loneliness or outbursts of anger. Those who struggle with PTSD may feel worried, guilty, or sad much of the time.

- Selective mutism

Selective mutism (SM) refers to a disorder in which the patient can usually speak but does not speak in certain situations or when facing certain people. Selective mutism is usually accompanied by shyness or social anxiety. Patients with selective mutism often choose not to speak, and when they do, it regularly leads to shame and even mental punishment. Selective mutism affects approximately 0.8% of people at some point in their life.

SYMPTOMS OF AN ANXIETY ATTACK

Symptoms can vary between person to person, but an anxiety crisis is considered to have occurred when more than one of the following symptoms occur:

- Palpitations or increased heart rate (tachycardia).
- Choking sensation, with rapid breathing.
- Chest tightness.
- Fear or panic; literally feeling like dying.
- Sweating or chills
- Tremors
- Nausea or abdominal discomfort.

- Dizziness or even fainting
- Feeling of unreality.
- Numbness or tingling sensation.

REASONS PEOPLE ARE ANXIOUS

Biological factors: These include genetic influences and physiological factors. Many have physical diseases or biological dysfunctions, which may cause anxiety, solely due to birth defects. Although this is not the only cause of anxiety, it is common that the patient's anxiety is caused by physical factors, such as hyperthyroidism and adrenal tumors.

Psychological factors: These include cognition, emotion, etc. These play a very important role in people's anxiety. If someone interprets ambiguous or even benign events as a crisis, believing that bad things will always befall them, it is likely to cause severe anxiety.

Social environmental factors: These include dense cities, crowded living spaces, environmental pollution, stress, and excessive work pressure. It also includes natural and man-made disasters, social unrest, work, economy, marriage, family, housing, illness, and loneliness. No matter what kind of disaster occurs, a healthy body will always produce tension, panic, and defense. Such a physiological order is an indispensable response. For example, when we see a poisonous snake, we don't need to think about it. Our body's first awareness is to escape; standing in a dangerous spot at a high place will stop your legs from moving forward; you cannot help it. Physiological imbalance produces a huge protective force that allows us to escape danger, but also makes us anxious.

HOW MINDFULNESS CAN IMPROVE OUR HEALTH

Developing our consciousness so that it is fuller brings us great health benefits. Interest in mindfulness has been on the rise, not only at the street level but also at the academic level. As stated, research has shown that mindfulness's continued practice helps us use our mind as an instrument that provides us with the calm and balance that we need so much in our lives.

We identify with our thoughts to the point of interpreting more than there is. Our mind races ahead and we worry about what might happen. We presuppose both situations and people automatically and without awareness, which leads us to distort reality. And the worst thing is that we end up suffering from this redundant blight and generating emotions that we cannot get out of until we become aware of the mechanism that has caused them to reach you. At some point we all feel identified with this situation.

We are continually generating thoughts, feelings and emotions that turn into discomfort and suffering. We justify it with what happens around us, but the truth is that the responsibility of the mental mechanism that we use is ours, and no one else's.

Our mind is a powerful instrument, and with it, we can destroy ourselves or contribute to our personal development. This depends on how we use it. Meditation through mindfulness teaches us to use our minds to expand our consciousness and develop in health, helping us avoid unnecessary suffering that takes over our lives.

THE BENEFITS OF MINDFULNESS FOR OUR HEALTH

Meditation helps us develop mindfulness, but what is mindfulness for? As research has shown us, the answer is that mindfulness gives us an effective method to manage our emotions, thoughts, and reactions. When we learn to manage these series of vital matters, we prepare ourselves to face situations, which can usually cause us to fall into depression, anxiety and deep discomfort.

By developing this capacity that every human being possesses, mindfulness, we develop attitudes that make us accept our vulnerabilities, our fragility and sensitivity. This acceptance supposes a change for our mind, which immediately predisposes itself to stop fighting against what we feel and what we experience. This is what truly frees our mind to focus on the present.

When we focus our mind on the present, thanks to acceptance and self-knowledge, we learn to connect with ourselves, to develop our self-knowledge.

What benefits does this have for our health? Inevitably our health is influenced by our mental attitude. Through this mindfulness attitude of mind, we learn to control stress and anxiety.

Stress and anxiety are a product of how we are managing our mind. It is something that, unfortunately, the vast majority of people suffer regularly. Many diseases and mental disorders are associated with the levels of anxiety and stress in our body. We increase our cortisol (a hormone that is released in our body in response to stress), and its effects can be devastating to our health.

Through mindfulness and the mental attitude that we learn to develop, it has been proven that cortisol levels decrease in situations we go through in our day to day life that typically cause its levels to increase. It makes perfect sense when we indicate that our health and our discomfort do not depend directly on the circumstances. Our health often depends on ourselves, on how we have learned to manage thoughts and emotions in certain situations.

IMPROVING OUR EMOTIONAL HEALTH

Emotional health, as research has shown, is an indicator of both physical and mental health. Through mindfulness, it is possible to develop emotional intelligence to better manage our emotions, with what this implies.

If you learn to manage your emotions, it is assured that self-knowledge, care and concentration will also be improved. This is one of the fundamental pillars of personal development and growth. That is why it is not surprising that many books, articles, conferences and courses are published today on this topic that is flourishing; its importance has been demonstrated.

A study carried out by the University of Toronto showed that people who use continuous mindfulness practice develop considerably greater emotional control than people who do not incorporate this practice in their lives. Obtaining greater emotional control means facing situations without finding that they affect us more than necessary. The goal is not to eliminate emotions that we dislike. What emotional regulation helps us is to adjust those emotions, so as not to over-amplify them and not to repress them, since both extremes are dangerous and cause us unceasing suffering.

People who develop their emotional intelligence do not eliminate any emotion; they learn to experience, accept, and attend to them in the most appropriate way as to not affect their inner world. The mental calm that is exercised thanks to mindfulness also has a lot to do with this. In order to attend to ourselves correctly and to be able to listen to ourselves, we need first to calm our mind, removing it from all the mental noise that contaminates our emotions and our behavior.

By improving our emotional health, we are helping to improve all aspects of our health, since emotions mediate in many biological processes, influencing both greater well-being and some diseases' appearance and effects. By learning to manage our emotions, we avoid our self-destruction.

Increasingly, experts from the world of medicine and psychology insist on the importance of taking care of our mind, as proposed by the Create Health method. We must be aware that to live a healthy life we also need to nourish ourselves properly and actively do things that contribute to our overall wellbeing.

HOW TO DEAL WITH INSOMNIA AND GET DEEP, RESTFUL SLEEP, ACCORDING TO SCIENCE

The hygiene of sleep refers to those factors that favour the quality of our night's rest, which also includes our habits and customs during wakefulness.

Let us explore the leading causes that trigger undesirable insomnia, and also investigate some recommendations backed by science that you can incorporate to say goodbye, once and for all, to sleepless nights.

THE RELATIONSHIP BETWEEN YOUR HEALTH, YOUR HAPPINESS AND YOUR SLEEP

Sleep is one of the most important factors in living a healthy and fulfilling life.

At the health level, good quality of sleep allows for psychobiological growth, balances our emotional processes and optimizes the defense systems that keep us healthy against the threat of viruses, bacteria and other infectious agents.

On the other hand, poor sleep has a multitude of adverse health effects and can lead to undesirable sleep disorders, among which is the infamous insomnia, which currently affects hundreds of millions of people around the world.

But in addition to insomnia, sleep deprivation has pernicious effects on our body weight. People are often unaware of this, but our body relies on REM sleep to regulate appetite. During this phase of deep and restorative sleep, cortisol (the main stress hormone) is suppressed. When we don't sleep well, our cortisol levels go up. This can cause a change in hormones and peptides that regulate appetite, resulting in imbalances such as voracity and uncontrolled hunger.

One study showed that at its most extreme, a single night of sleep deprivation can equate to six months on a diet high in saturated fat. The researchers found that a single night of sleep deprivation decreased insulin sensitivity by 33%, while six months of a high-fat diet decreased it by 21%. Insulin resistance is a condition in which the body does not use insulin efficiently to move glucose from the blood into the cells, and is a hallmark of both type 2 diabetes and prediabetes.

But in addition to the physical aspect, poor sleep makes it difficult for us to feel happy and full.

You see, negative stimuli are processed by the amygdala, while the hippocampus processes positive or neutral memories. Sleep deprivation hits the hippocampus harder than the amygdala. The result is that, people who lack sleep are more aware of their dark memories than their pleasant memories, and this causes them to feel depressed, worried and anxious during the day.

In addition, lack of sleep also leads to a complete lack of emotional control. Recent research from Tel Aviv University, published in the Journal of Neuroscience, identified the neurological mechanisms that associate poor sleep with emotional imbalance.

Lack of sleep causes us to lose neutrality, that is, the ability to remain equanimous in the face of what we perceive and experience. This causes an impulsive reaction to our thoughts and our experiences:

- The mental storm is unleashed.
- We enter into internal chaos that we also transfer outwardly.
- Even the slightest of stimuli is perceived in a threatening way.

You must understand exactly what is happening to you and why it is happening in order to begin to solve the problem, so let us start with the most basic: sleep deprivation and insomnia are not limited to night time problems.

Yes, they manifest at night, but the root of the problem is in the hours of light.

THE REAL CAUSE OF THE PROBLEM

Perhaps you have noticed that when you go to bed you not only have trouble sleeping, but your mind puts in front of you a multitude of thoughts that keep you alert: worries about the future (including worrying about what will happen the next day if you can't rest tonight), memories that disturb you and scenes that lead to nothing but internal suffocation and discomfort. That is, your mind is not calm, but rather the opposite: it is agitated and nervous.

This mental agitation is not the result of a random process. When you go to bed, your mind is scrambled because your nervous system is in threat mode. Why is our threat mode active? Because it has been active all day.

During the day, you have been under great mental tension, turning your fears and worries over and over. But you have obligations, so naturally, you have carried on with your life without too many impediments. Yet, now that you want to sleep, your nervous system is not working.

When you go to bed, your mind is full of thoughts that rob you of sleep. It is important that you understand that they were always there. During the day, you had a head full of them. They didn't magically appear now that you want to sleep. Your nervous system has been so alert throughout the day that it now continues to feel threatened and does not want to fall into the realm of sleep.

If we are under threat, the last thing the nervous system wants is for you to fall asleep. Evolutionarily, it doesn't make much sense to fall asleep if there's a lion stalking us. And for your nervous system, all those negative thoughts are threats as real as the lion. Each thought carries information through the brain circuits and has the same neurological weight as the events and situations we experience. So as long as your mind is flooded with negative thoughts, your nervous system will not allow you to fall asleep.

If you want your mind to support your rest at night, you must get it out of those many hours of mental turmoil. You must learn to get out of the inner chaos that keeps the threat mode of your nervous system active throughout the day, not just at night, and fortunately, it is easier than you think.

www.ingramcontent.com/pod-product-compliance
Lightning Source LLC
Chambersburg PA
CBHW070223180726
47999CB00017B/1954